HAL LEONARD

UKULELE METHOD

BLUES UKULELE

BY DAVE RUBIN

T0071667

To access audio visit:
www.halleonard.com/mylibrary

Enter Code
6895-9485-5967-3675

Ukulele in cover photo courtesy of Lil' Rev

ISBN 978-1-4584-2271-2

7777 W. BLUEMOUND RD. P.O. BOX 13819 MILWAUKEE, WI 53213

In Australia Contact:
Hal Leonard Australia Pty. Ltd.
4 Lentara Court
Cheltenham, Victoria, 3192 Australia
Email: ausadmin@halleonard.com.au

Visit Hal Leonard Online at **www.halleonard.com**

DEDICATION AND ACKNOWLEDGMENTS

I would like to dedicate this book to all the great string bands of the early 20th century that laid the groundwork for the blues that followed, while simultaneously creating a glorious body of work. Thanks to my friend Edward Komara, former Blues Archivist at Ole Miss and current Music Librarian at SUNY Potsdam, N.Y., and renowned ukulele expert Dan "Cool Hand Duke" Scanlan.

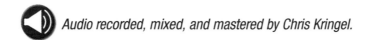 *Audio recorded, mixed, and mastered by Chris Kringel.*

CONTENTS

INTRODUCTION

Welcome to the *Hal Leonard Blues Ukulele Method*. The goal of this book is to provide a comprehensive introduction to playing a wide variety of blues on the ukulele. While experienced guitarists will find it immediately accessible, beginners on either the guitar or ukulele will be swinging, shuffling, and improvising in no time as they progress through all of the most important blues techniques. While there are several varieties of ukuleles, this book is geared toward the standard soprano model.

HISTORY OF THE UKULELE IN THE BLUES

The birth of the ukulele begins on the Portuguese island of Madeira with the "braguinha," which arrived from the mainland in 1854, along with the larger "rajao." The former is tuned D–G–B–D, while the latter is D–G–C–A–A. When 400 Portuguese immigrants landed in Hawaii in 1879 to work in the sugar cane fields, musicians among their numbers brought both instruments along. One man in particular, Joao Fernandes, was so happy to be there that he immediately grabbed a braguinha and began to play for the delighted islanders. Through the skills of Portuguese craftsmen who had also made the trek and could fashion instruments, the two originals would evolve into the ukulele, with the G–C–E–A tuning derived from the rajao, and its smaller size based on the braguinha. The Hawaiian word "ukulele" translates roughly to "jumping flea" and is generally accepted as the basis of the name, though there are several other theories, including one that suggests the meaning as "the gift that came from here," from "uku" (gift or reward), and "lele" (to come).

Hawaiian music that incorporated the diminutive stringed instrument was first introduced to an American audience at the World's Fairs of 1895 and 1901 in Chicago and Buffalo, respectively, and at the Lewis and Clark Exposition in 1905. However, it was the Panama Pacific International Exposition of 1915 in San Francisco, where a guitar and ukulele quartet entertained in the Hawaiian Pavilion, that ignited the craze that swept the mainland. By the 1920s, it was regularly appearing onstage and in popular recordings with early stars Roy Smeck and Cliff "Ukulele Ike" Edwards.

Its role in the history of prewar blues, however, remains a sidebar to the story, most likely due to its low volume output compared to the banjo, guitar, fiddle, and mandolin. Clarence Conaway accompanied Clara Smith on the ukulele, and Sterling Conaway played it behind Helen Gross in 1924. The Pebbles, comprised of Baxter White and Alphonsus Agee, recorded half a dozen sides in 1926–27 featuring the ukulele. Fletcher Henderson, the legendary bandleader and arranger in the 1920s and 1930s most known for playing the piano, also played ukulele behind a long list of singers in the prewar era.

Bob Fuller, better known for playing the clarinet as a sideman, also dabbled on the ukulele in the 1920s. Harry "Ukulele" Mays was sideman to Danny Small and a member of the Two of Spades with Herbert Leonard (harmonica and washboard). "Ukulele Bob" Williams recorded extensively from 1924–29, including behind Ethel Ridley, while Samuel "Fat" Westmoreland was one of the few blues singers to accompany himself in the 1920s, including the unreleased "Real Estate Mama" and "Dreamin' Blues." Virgil Van Cleve recorded with Ethel Waters on "Pickininny Blues" in 1925, and Robert Ward played guitar and ukulele with the Four Southern Singers, probably recording with the latter instrument on "Hambone Am Sweet" in 1933.

Charlie Burse (1901–65)—known as "Uke Kid Burse" and who also played banjo, guitar, and mandolin—enjoyed some renown in Will Shade's Memphis Jug Band, starting in 1928. Burse and Shade would play together long after the jug band stopped recording in 1934, while Burse would lead the progressive Memphis Mudcats jug band for a short spell, beginning in 1939.

Thanks to TV star Arthur Godfrey, a second ukulele boom occured in the 1950s and lasted into the 1960s due to the growing interest in folk music and the desire of many young people to make their own music. The ukulele's size and easy playability proved it to be the perfect entrance-level instrument. Yet a third boom arrived in the 1990s and continues unabated. Hawaiian star Israel Kamakawiwo'ole played a major role after a medley of his recordings found its way into movies and television. Perhaps most influential has been Jake Shimabukuro, a true virtuoso of jazz, rock, and pop music. His live solo chord-melody version of the Beatles' "While My Guitar Gently Weeps," posted on YouTube in 2006 with almost 10 million views to date, along with Queen's "Bohemian Rhapsody" (among others), not only sent uke players scrambling to the "woodshed," but likely many guitarists as well.

It remains to be seen whether a blues uke star of the magnitude of Jake will emerge, but if the number of uke players posting excellent blues performances online are any indication, it's only a matter of time.

THE TUNING

While the uke's tuning may initially baffle guitarists, it's actually a tuning relative to strings 1–3 on the guitar, but down an interval of a 4th. So, instead of E, B, and G, on the uke, it's A, E, and C. String 4 is tuned to G, as would normally be expected with the 4th-higher routine established thus far, but an octave higher than normal, so it actually sounds higher in pitch than strings 3 and 2. This is called "re-entrant tuning." From low to high (G–C–E–A), the open strings sound the melody "My dog has fleas."

The tuning clearly relates the strongest to the keys of C (5th, root, 3rd, and 6th, low to high) and G (root, 4th, 6th, and 2nd). However, all keys may be accessed, including the common blues guitar keys of E and A.

CHORD COMPING

"Comping" is short for "accompaniment" and usually refers to the act of playing chords in support of a singer or soloist. In the blues style, it's helpful to familiarize yourself with as many chord variations as possible. As most songs will take place in the standard 12-bar format, and many make use of only the I, IV, and V chords, every bit of variety you can muster is welcome!

12-BAR BLUES

The 12-bar form is the standard blues form that's heard in countless blues classics, not to mention pop, rock, country, and jazz songs. It's one of the first song forms that many players learn, and you'll no doubt play it hundreds of times (if not thousands) during your lifetime.

A "slow drag" with the "fast change" in the "people's key" of C is an excellent place to start playing ukulele blues. Open strings on a guitar always add vibrancy, volume, and sustain, and these qualities are to be sought after on the uke whenever possible. Observe that a classic Robert Johnson diminished turnaround has been utilized in measures 11–12. The result provides authenticity, as well as extra harmony and rhythmic variety—a worthy goal in all uke blues.

Performance Tip: The pick-hand thumb may be employed for strumming the chords with downstrokes, while the thumb and index finger, low to high, access the turnaround pattern.

TRACK 1

Slow Blues ♩. = 72

5

Depending on the key and the desired effect, **barre chords** can be an efficient comping tool for building a sturdy harmonic foundation. Notice that the real beauty lies in the ease with which the change from a major triad to a dominant 7th chord may be made.

Performance Tip: Barre across all four strings with the index finger in order to maintain a decent arch to the ring and middle fingers, low to high, for the major triads.

TRACK 2

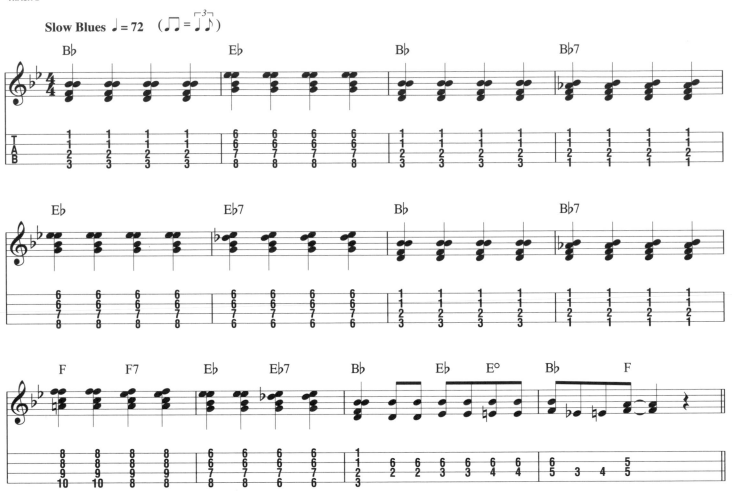

A swinging Texas shuffle with the "Charleston beat" provides a dandy opportunity to expand the chord palette to include hip dominant voicings. Check out measures 7–8, the I (A) chord, where common tones and voicings that ascend in pitch contribute to increased forward motion. Likewise, the transition from the I chord in measure 8 to the V (E) chord in measure 9 is enhanced by a common tone (E) and "voice leading" on strings 3 and 2.

Performance Tip: Except for the D13 in measures 6 and 11 and the A7 voicings in measures 7–8, all the chords employ the middle finger on string 4, making for smooth, efficient harmonic changes.

TRACK 3

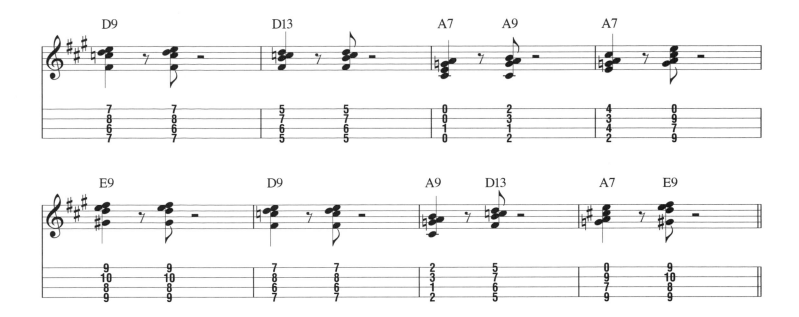

Substitute chords and alternate voicings can really dress up a uke blues accompaniment. Similar to the "Stormy Monday" progression, the following example "progresses" forward with chord voicings in measures 4–6, over the I (C) and IV (F) changes, that ascend in pitch. In measures 7–8, the chords ascend and descend with substitutions of Dm7 (ii) and Em7 (iii) in place of the C7 (I), with the E♭m7 (♭iii) acting as a passing chord. Note that the D♭maj7 (♭II) in measure 10 is a substitute for the G7 (V), as heard prominently in the Allman Brothers Band version of "Stormy Monday" on *Live at Fillmore East*.

Performance Tip: For a hip move that is efficient and also looks flashy, utilize the thumb to fret the A♭ (♭3rd) note on string 4 for the Fm change in measure 11.

TRACK 4

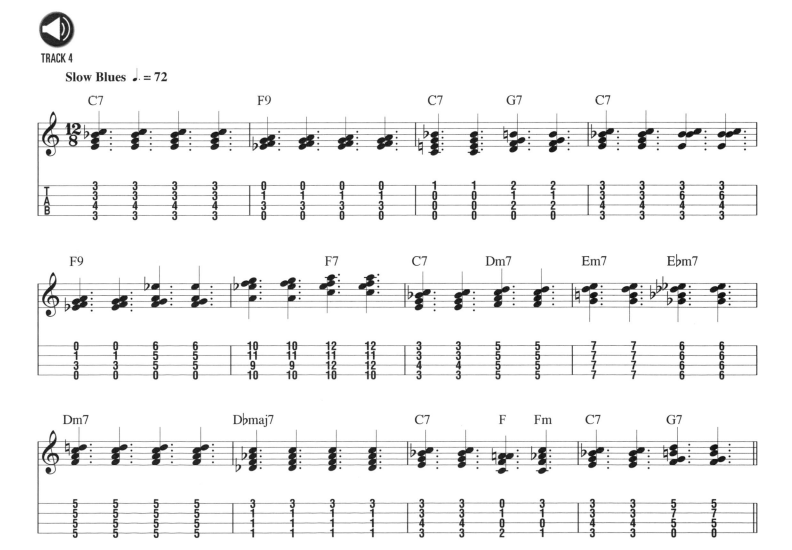

Texas swing like the music of Bob Wills and the Texas Playboys in the 1930s and 1940s often featured guitarist Eldon Shamblin utilizing sweet 6ths, which were also found in the Kansas City swing of Count Basie and other jazz bands in the 1930s. Later on, rockabilly cats like Cliff Gallup with Gene Vincent and Bill Haley with his Comets also would incorporate the distinctive tonality. Take note of the close voicings of the I (G6) and IV (C7) chords, as well as the extensive use of diminished chords, for a "jazzier" feel. Also observe the I (G)–ii (Am)–iii (Bm7)–VI (E7#9) changes in measures 7–8, over the I chord.

Performance Tip: Due to the straightforward rhythm throughout, the pick-hand thumb may be used as a "pick" to down-strum each chord.

TRACK 5

8

Sweet 6th chords lead logically to dominant 7th voicings for the best of both jazz and blues, while also peacefully coexisting and often being interchanged. The more prominent aspects that push this progression in the most sophisticated direction, however, are the many substitute chords in measures 7–8, over the I (D) chord change, and measures 9–10, over the ii (Em)–V (A) change. Check out the diminished chords in the former that smoothly connect the I to the ii. In the latter, the ii chord in measure 9 descends fluidly in pitch through measure 10, with the E♭maj7 substitution for Gm (iv) enabling the B♭ note on string 4 to function as a common tone in the E♭maj7, Gm7, and C7 voicings. In addition, the B♭ moves down by a half step to the A note in the D7 chord of measure 11.

Performance Tip: Barre the D6 chord with your index finger in measures 1, 3, and 7, as well as the G6 in measure 5. This approach will allow easy access to the dominant 7th voicings that follow by adding the middle finger to string 1.

TRACK 6

9

8-BAR BLUES

Surprisingly, perhaps, far more harmonic variations appear in 8-bar blues than in 12-bar blues. As seen in the following progression, a common denominator often found in 8-bar blues is that chord changes tend to be in two-measure chunks, rather than four or one. Two other characteristics often found in 8-bar blues are the quick change to the V (D7) chord in measure 1 and the I (G7), VI (E7), II (A7), and V chords in measures 5–6, which substantially help to propel the progression forward.

Performance Tip: Efficient fret-hand fingerings for measures 5–6 would be, low to high: middle, index, and ring for the G7; move the index finger to string 4 for E7; move the index over one string while lifting the middle and ring fingers for A7; and finally, barring across fret 2 with the index and adding the middle finger to string 1 for D7.

TRACK 7

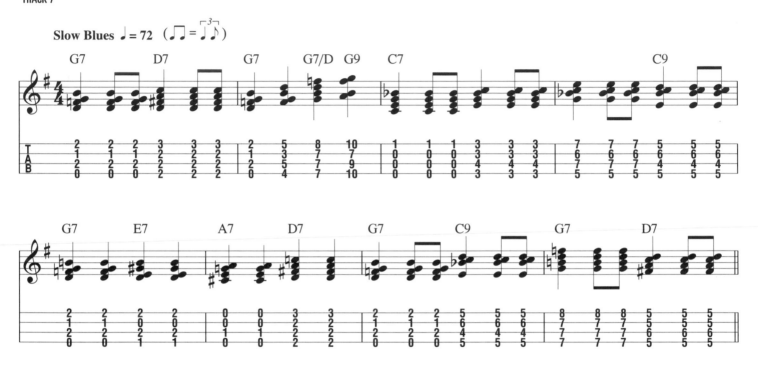

This classic 8-bar blues progression is based on "Key to the Highway." Generally credited to Big Bill Broonzy (1940 and 1941), the song has been famously covered by Little Walter (1958) and Eric Clapton and Duane Allman on *Layla...* (1970). In addition, Sam "the Sham" Samudio recorded it in 1970 for an album that featured Duane Allman on one track. As is important with most rhythm work, and particularly in the blues where momentum and forward motion is so highly valued, note the close voicings and common tones in measures 1–4.

Performance Tip: Use the fret-hand ring finger on string 1 in measures 1, 2, and 3, switching to the index finger in measure 4.

TRACK 8

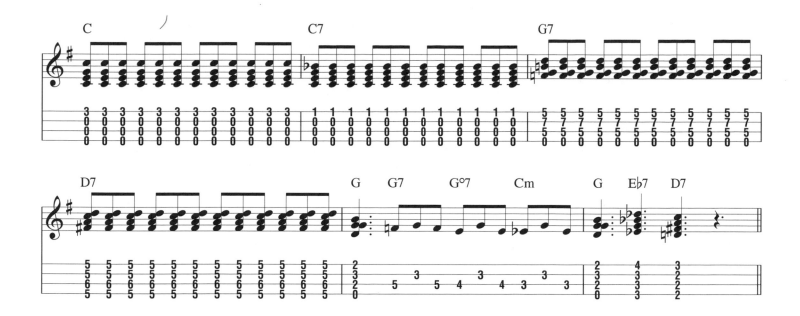

MINOR BLUES

Minor key slow blues songs are considered the most dramatic, if not melodramatic, of all blues music, and no less so on the ukulele. In the next example, observe the classic descending chord sequence in measures 7–8 over the i (Cm) change. Stevie Wonder featured it prominently in a pop setting with his song "Don't You Worry 'Bout a Thing" (1973), though it goes back much further in time. Similarly, the turnaround in measures 11–12 incorporates the Cm sequence with resolution to the V (G7) chord. Also notice measure 10, where the iv (Fm) change substitutes for the ♭VI (A♭) chord on beats 1 and 2, as heard on Led Zeppelin's "Since I've Been Loving You" (1970).

Performance Tip: In measures 7–8, barre all four strings with the index finger and descend string 4 with the ring and middle fingers, leaving the barre for the Cm7 voicing. For the Cm6 chord, barre strings 3–1 with the ring finger and place the index finger on string 4 at fret 2.

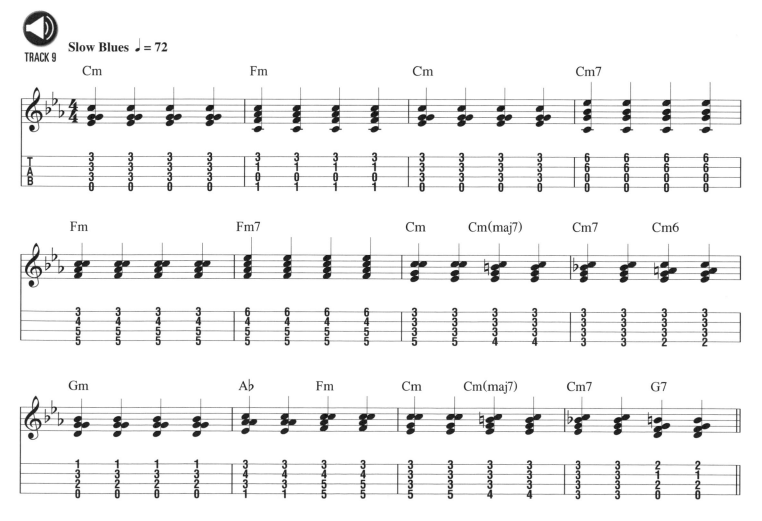

Similar to "Riders on the Storm" by the Doors (1971), the following progression is appropriately melancholy, as well as dramatic. The Allman Brothers Band utilized the same sequence in the key of C, rather than G, for their classic "Whipping Post" (1969 and 1971). The voicings require significant changes of fingerings. This technical challenge often occurs on the ukulele due to the re-entrant tuning, as well as the limited number of strings.

Performance Tip: In measures 1 and 2, low to high, use the fret-hand ring, middle, and index fingers for Em; the ring, pinky, middle, and index for F♯m; and the middle, ring, pinky, and index for G. However, for the G chord, you may want to try a significantly easier fingering by barring your ring finger across the bottom three strings and fretting string 1 with your index finger. The only catch is that this requires you to bend your ring finger knuckle backward a little bit so string 1 can ring through. This is a handy fretting trick for many uke chords if you're able to do it!

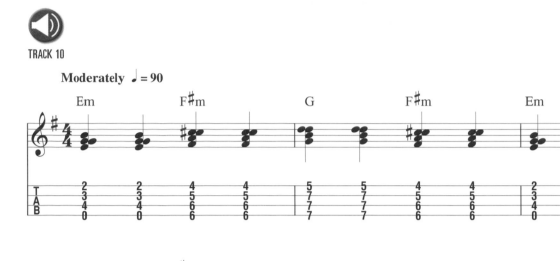

TRACK 10

Moderately ♩ = 90

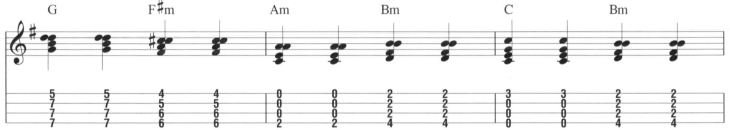

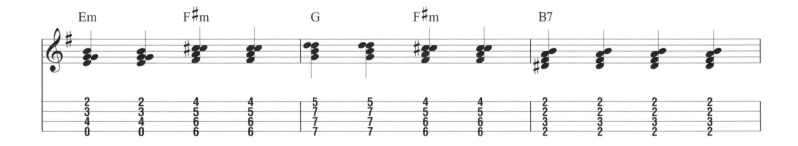

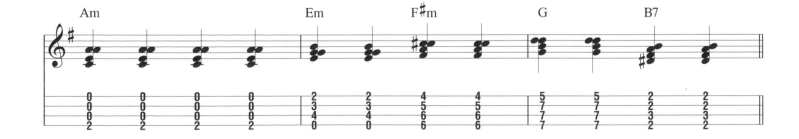

BOOGIE RHYTHMS

Boogie rhythms on string instruments are mostly adapted from piano patterns and make excellent accompaniments to vocals and solos alike. They can be extremely simple and repetitive or dressed up a bit. In htis chapter, we'll look at several different examples that suit the ukulele well.

While open-string boogie rhythms on the guitar lay best in the keys of E and A, the key of C is the most accessible on the ukulele. Notice in the following example that, while an open-string position is not available for the IV (F) chord, one is available for the V (G) chord but was not used in order to maintain a consistent sound on the same strings between the IV and V changes.

Performance Tip: For the IV and V changes, utilize the fret-hand index, ring, and pinky fingers, with the pinky handling the 6th and ♭7th notes.

TRACK 11

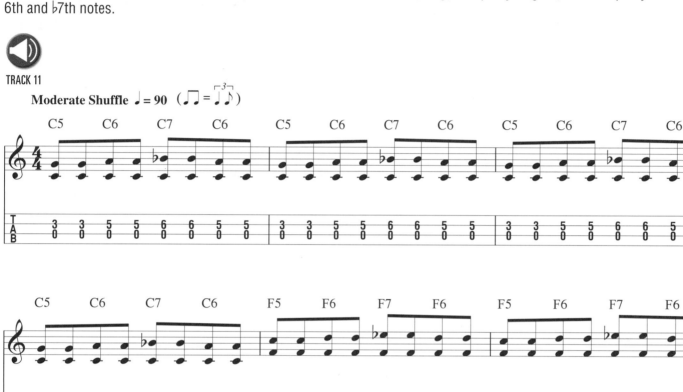

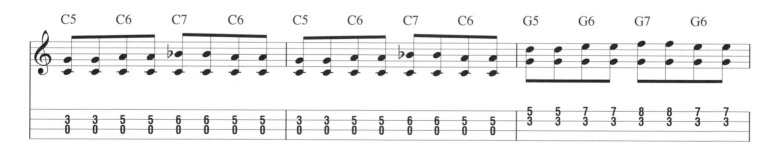

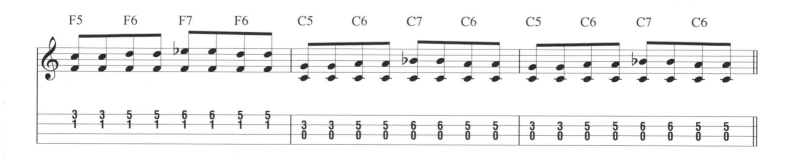

The open-string position for the I (G) chord functions as a boogie pattern, but having the G string sounding higher in pitch than the 5th (D) creates a different sonic result than expected. Note also that a string skip is required for the V (D) change, though the sound that is produced is typical.

Performance Tip: Employ the pick-hand thumb and index fingers to pluck the strings, while using the fret-hand index and ring fingers to fret the notes for the V change.

TRACK 12

Though A is one of the bedrock keys in blues guitar, on the ukulele it requires some very minimal finger "gymnastics" to play common "cut boogie" patterns.

Performance Tip: Observe that the exact same right- and left-hand fingerings that were used for the V chord (D) in the previous figure may be utilized for the I (A) and IV (D) changes here. For the V (E) chord, however, anchor the fret-hand ring finger at fret 4 of string 3 and employ the index and pinky fingers for the 5th, 6th, and ♭7th notes on string 1.

TRACK 13

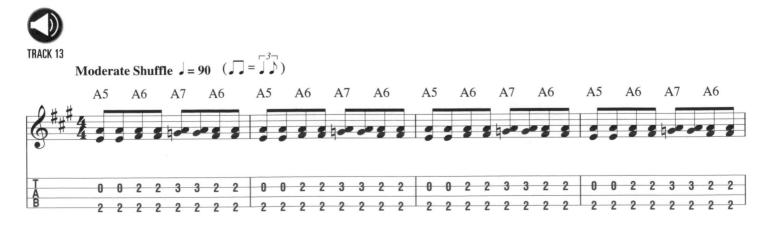

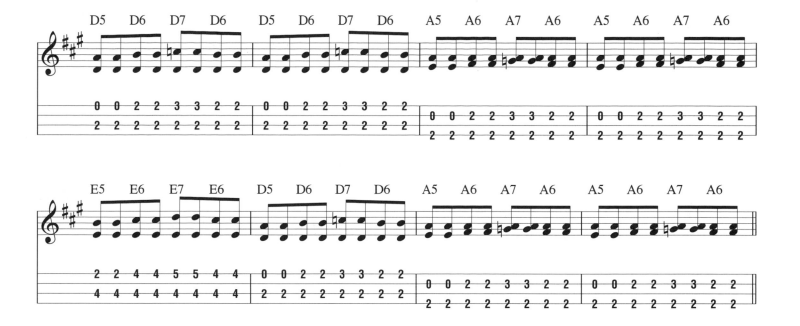

Despite the lack of bass-string "growl" for the I (E) chord, the key of E is still a useful and important key for blues on the uke.

Performance Tip: The fingerings for the IV (A) and V (B) chords coincide with the ones in Track 13, though the V chord is on strings 4 and 2, instead of 3 and 1.

TRACK 14

Moderate Shuffle ♩ = 90

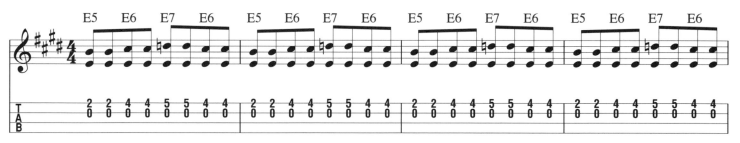

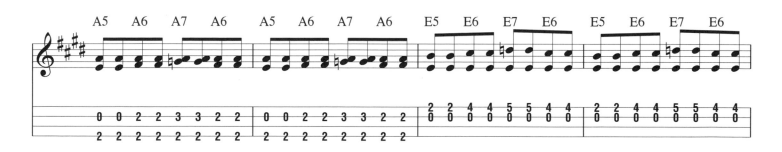

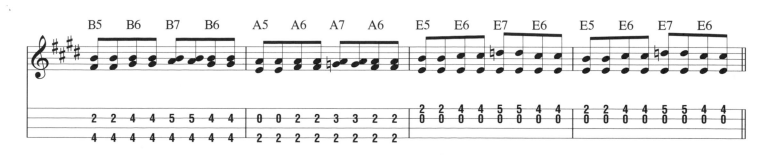

15

"Boogie on down" in D.

Performance Tip: For the I (D) chord, utilize the fingering from the IV (D) chord in Track 13, the I (G) chord in Track 12 for the IV (G) chord, and the I (A) chord in Track 13 for the V (A) chord change.

TRACK 15

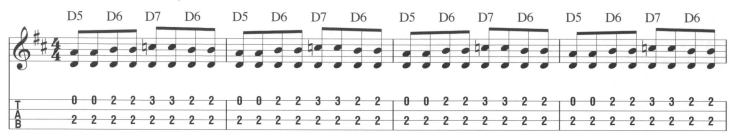

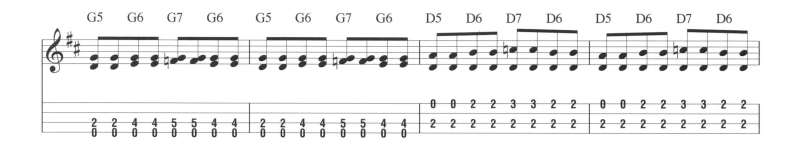

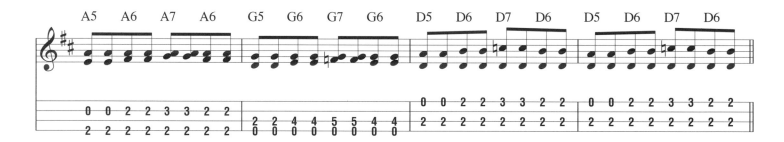

The next step in the evolution of hip boogie patterns involves embellishment with bass notes to help goose the progressions forward.

Performance Tip: For the I (C) chord, access the minor 3rd (E♭) and major 3rd (E) notes with the fret-hand middle and ring fingers, respectively, while keeping your index finger planted on the G note. For the IV (F) and V (G) chords, the pinky may be used for both notes (A♭ to A and B♭ to B, respectively).

TRACK 16

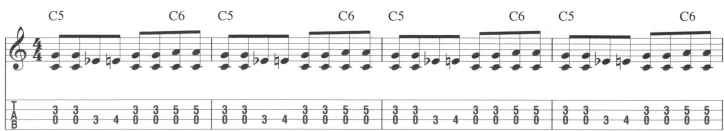

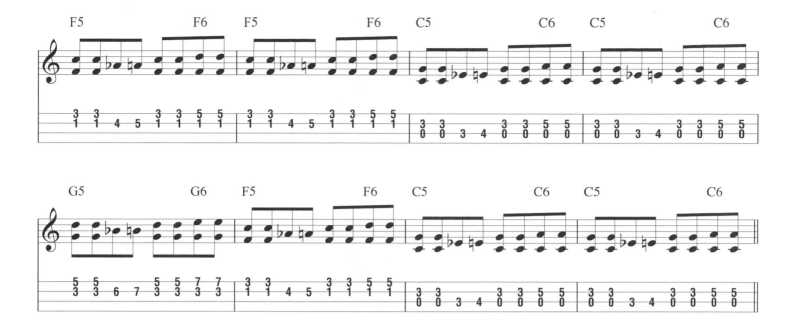

A consonant triplet from the major pentatonic scale containing the 5th, 6th, and root notes relative to each chord change adds a sweet snatch of melody on the tail end of each measure to dress up the following boogie pattern.

Performance Tip: The IV (C) and V (D) chord triplets may be played with the fret-hand index and ring fingers, while the I (G) chord triplets will be best handled by an index-ring-middle fingering.

TRACK 17

Moderate Shuffle ♩ = 90

The concept of playing a major-pentatonic triplet on beat 4 of each measure creates an aura of subtle musical tension through the repetition of the same three notes. Be aware that the E, F#, and A notes function as the 5th, 6th, and root of the I (A) chord; the 9th, 3rd, and 5th of the IV (D) chord; and the root, 9th, and 4th of the V (E) chord. Significantly, the triplet in conjunction with the V chord in measure 9 creates tension to heighten anticipation to the I chord in measures 11–12.

Performance Tip: Hammer to the F# note with the fret-hand middle finger for each triplet.

TRACK 18

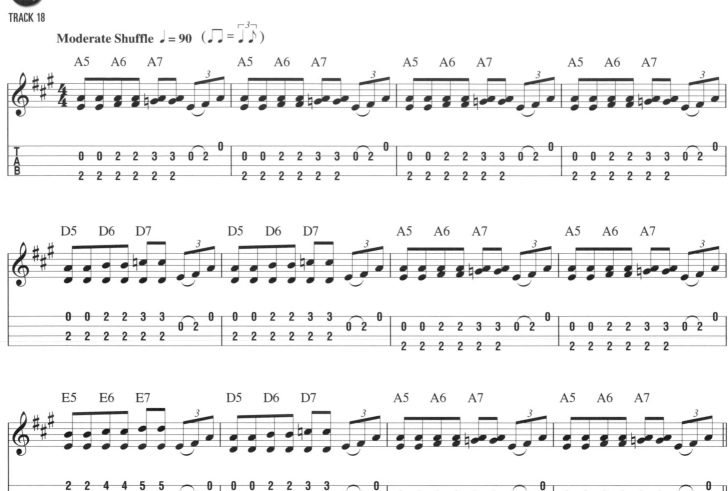

Shades of Jimmy Reed's "Big Boss Man" (1960) and Tommy Tucker's "Hi-Heel Sneakers" (1964) permeate this example via the triplet on beat 4 of each measure, which features the 6th, b7th, and 6th relative to each chord change.

Performance Tip: Regarding the triplets, employ the fret-hand ring and pinky fingers for the I (E) and V (B) chords and the middle and ring fingers for the IV (A) chord.

TRACK 19

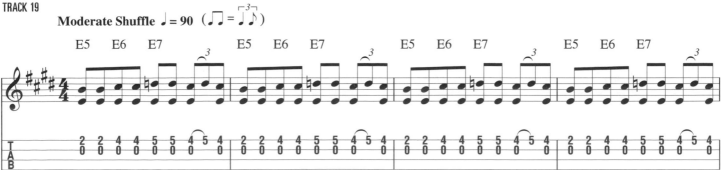

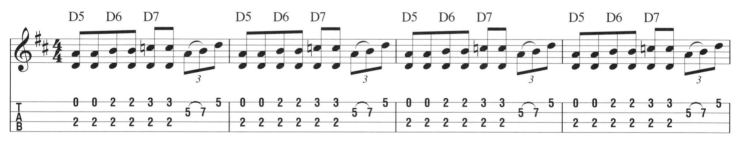

As in Track 17 (in the key of G), the 5th, 6th, and root notes relative to each chord change in the key of D occur on beat 4 of each measure.

Performance Tip: Likewise, utilize the fret-hand index and ring fingers for each triplet (and middle finger for the IV and V chords).

TRACK 20

Moderate Shuffle ♩ = 90 (♫ = triplet)

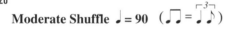

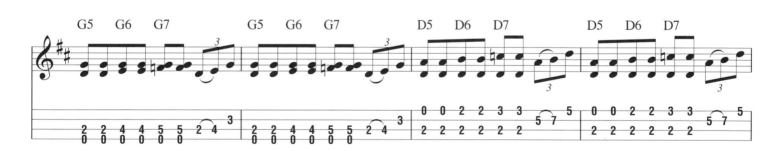

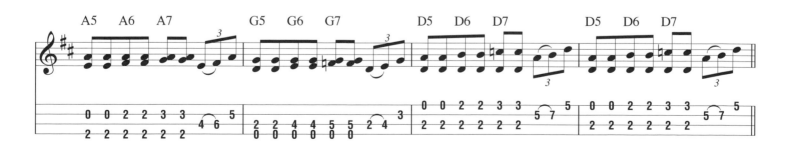

THE MINOR PENTATONIC SCALE

Due to the comparative tuning on strings 1–3, minor pentatonic "boxes" similar to the guitar may be played on the ukulele. Note that string 4 has been included, though the raised octave produces a unique sound and should be applied accordingly.

Performance Tip: The keys of C, G, A, E, and D are the most advantageous for the blues. However, any of the "boxes" that do not contain open strings may be moved to other keys as well.

◯ = Root

C Minor Pentatonic Scale (C–E♭–F–G–B♭)

G Minor Pentatonic Scale (G–B♭–C–D–F)

A Minor Pentatonic Scale (A–C–D–E–G)

E Minor Pentatonic Scale (E–G–A–B–D)

D Minor Pentatonic Scale (D–F–G–A–C)

THE MAJOR PENTATONIC SCALE

Aquick look will reveal why the keys of C and G are the easiest to access, as the fingerings get more convoluted in the other keys. Nonetheless, all keys are useful and will be worth the effort to learn in order to take full advantage of the potential of the instrument. B.B. King was one of the first to popularize the major pentatonic scale in the blues (on guitar), and his example has influenced countless other musicians.

Performance Tip: Notice that the first box in C contains a finger-friendly arrangement and moves easily up the neck into other keys.

◯ **= Root**

C Major Pentatonic Scale (C–D–E–G–A)

G Major Pentatonic Scale (G–A–B–D–E)

A Major Pentatonic Scale (A–B–C♯–E–F♯)

E Major Pentatonic Scale (E–F♯–G♯–B–C♯)

D Major Pentatonic Scale (D–E–F♯–A–B)

THE BLUES SCALE

Though the blues scale contains only one additional note, the ♭5th, compared to the minor pentatonic scale, that note considerably alters many of the fingerings. The "blue" note (the ♭5th) can often be comfortably fretted in two different positions—it's simply a matter of whether you want to briefly reach up or back out of position. The fingerings here represent suggestions, but feel free to tailor them to your taste if desired.

◯ = Root

C Blues Scale (C–E♭–F–G♭–G–B♭)

G Blues Scale (G–B♭–C–D♭–D–F)

A Blues Scale (A–C–D–E♭–E–G)

E Blues Scale (E–G–A–B♭–B–D)

D Blues Scale (D–F–G–A♭–A–C)

THE COMPOSITE BLUES SCALE

The most "sophisticated" of blues scales is a combination of the blues scale and the Mixolydian mode, though for practical reasons, it does not contain every single note from both. Like the major pentatonic, the composite blues scale has been a favorite of B.B. King as well as jazzy blues players, from T-Bone Walker to Billy Butler, Rick Holmstrom, Junior Watson, and beyond.

Performance Tip: Observe that all four fingers are required in each key, though they will rarely be played in sequence in the blues, as it will not often produce an idiomatic effect.

◯ = **Root**

C Composite Blues Scale (C–D–E♭–E–F–G–A–B♭)

G Composite Blues Scale (G–A–B♭–B–C–D–E–F)

A Composite Blues Scale (A–B–C–C♯–D–E–F♯–G)

E Composite Blues Scale (E–F♯–G–G♯–A–B–C♯–D)

D Composite Blues Scale (D–E–F–F♯–G–A–B–C)

STRING BENDING

Theoretically, any bends that could be executed on strings 1–3 on the guitar may be duplicated on the ukulele, and a quick perusal of the following examples in the keys of C, G, A, E, and D will confirm this.

Performance Tip: Be aware of two caveats when bending strings on the ukulele: the size of the instrument combined with nylon strings results in a short amount of sustain, so steady, significant pressure needs to be applied to get the strings to "sing" when bent and vibratoed. Likewise, the string tension is quite light, making it far too easy to overbend if you're not careful.

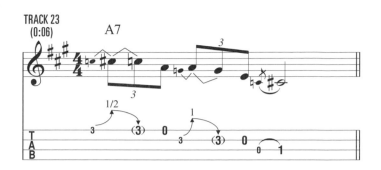

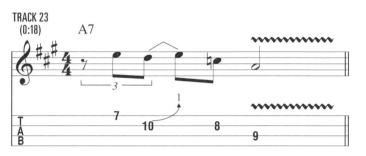

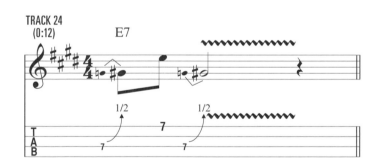

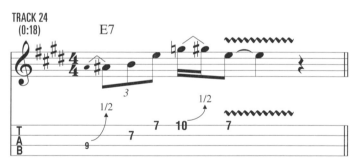

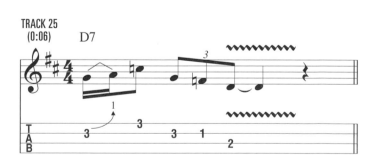

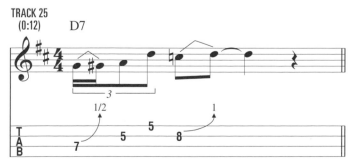

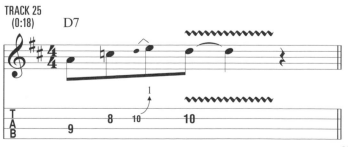

CLASSIC BLUES LICKS

As an extension of (and including) bending licks, the classic blues licks in the keys of C, G, A, E, and D are virtually identical to ones on strings 1–3 of the guitar. Of course, the few that include notes on string 4 present a different effect due to the tuning that is characteristic of the ukulele and should be considered as a unique improvisational tool.

Performance Tip: Though the notes that are played on string 4 may be accessed on string 1 as well, the proximity of string 4 to the lower notes produces a quicker and more fluid dynamic leap in register.

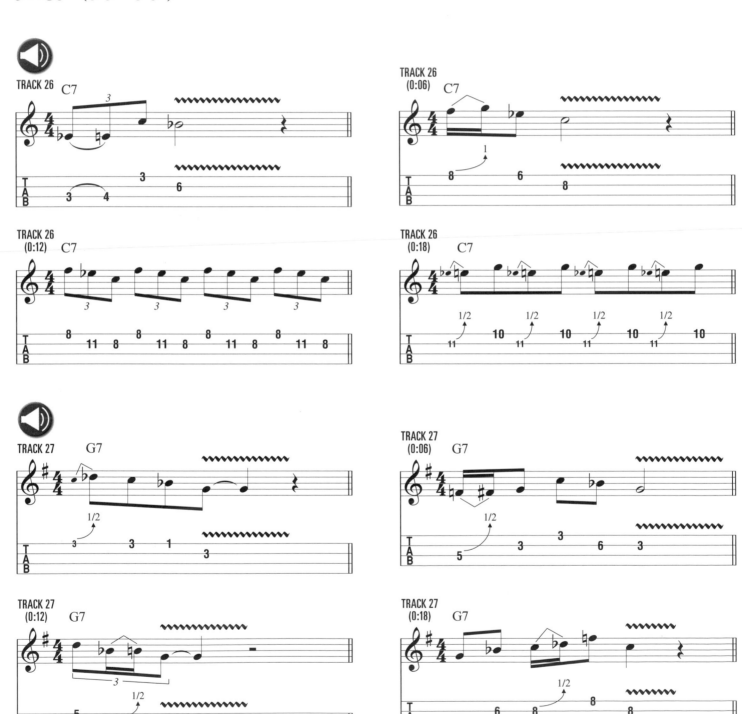

26

27

MIXOLYDIAN DOUBLE STOPS: 6THS

Double stops (or dyads) exist in that middle ground between single-note melodies and chords. As such, they may function as one or the other, or both. Given the relatively lightweight sound that is produced by single-note runs on the ukulele, the harmony provided by double stops can add considerable musical weight to the sound of the blues. Double stops voiced in "sweet" 6ths have been utilized extensively by blues guitarists, most notably by the legendary Freddie King in his classic instrumentals like "Hide Away," "The Stumble," and "Sad Nite Owl."

Performance Tip: Two efficient fret-hand fingerings (low to high) are recommended throughout: middle and index for the "diagonal" shapes and middle and ring for the "parallel" shapes.

 = **Root**

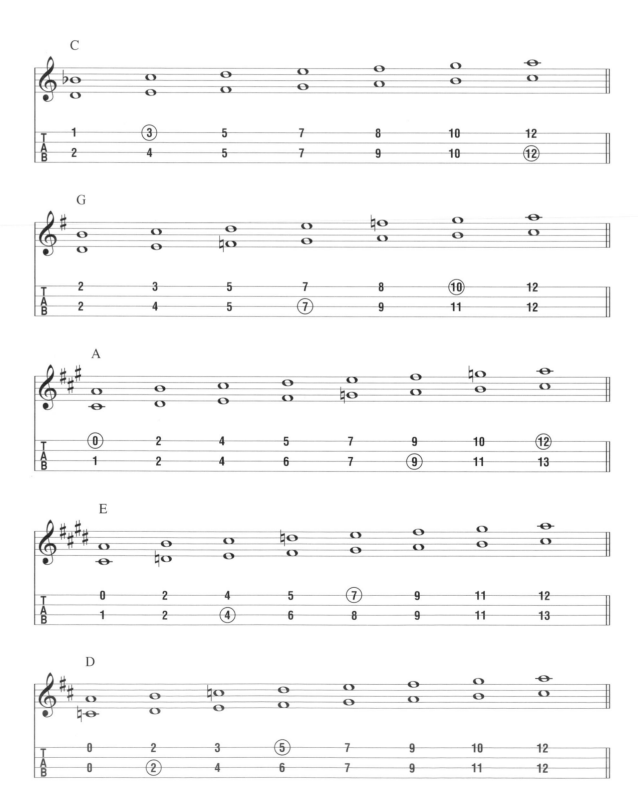

MIXOLYDIAN DOUBLE STOPS: 3RDS

Compared to 6ths, double stops voiced in 3rds are employed more regularly in rock, as well as in the blues. Perhaps it is their noticeably heavier, punchier sound. Or perhaps it's because 3rds are easier to play as opposed to 6ths, which contain a non-played "dead" string between the two notes.

Performance Tip: For the fret-hand fingerings, use a combination of middle and index, ring and index, or just the index as a small barre.

 = **Root**

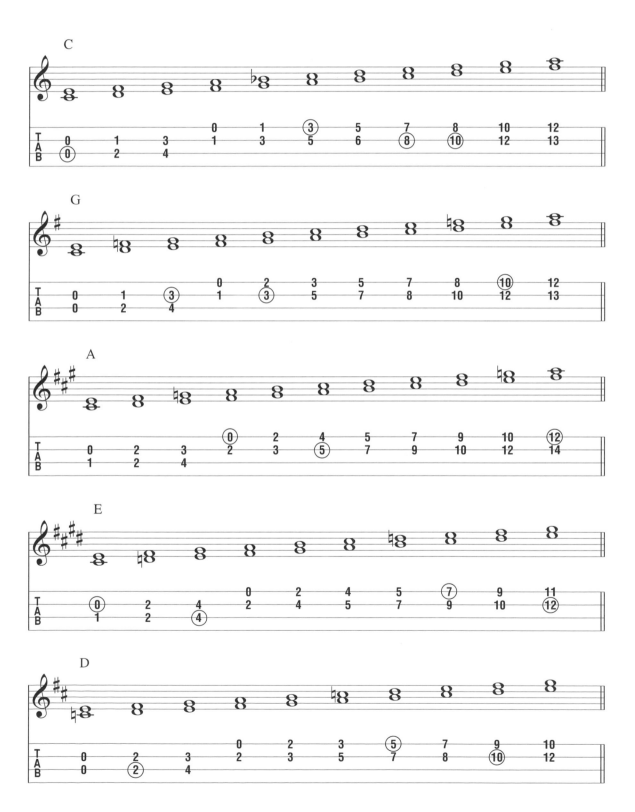

INTROS AND TURNAROUNDS

Propulsive intros and turnarounds have always been a hallmark of the stone blues musician and will bring ukulele blues to the appropriate level of authenticity. Observe that they usually consist of dyads in 6ths or 3rds, implying a moving harmony that descends (or ascends) from the I chord to an alternate voicing of the I chord and resolves to the V chord, creating momentum into the next chorus. As with most aspects of playing blues on the ukulele, the patterns change greatly from key to key—a characteristic that may be advantageously exploited for variety.

Performance Tip: Be aware that most of these descending patterns could be reversed for another type of anticipation that is generally perceived as more upbeat.

Slow Blues ♩ = 72

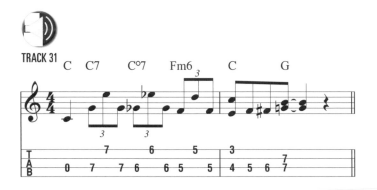

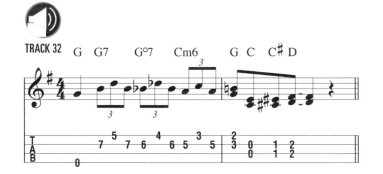

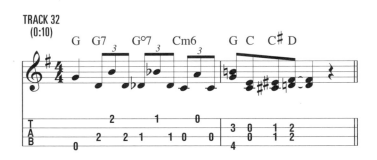

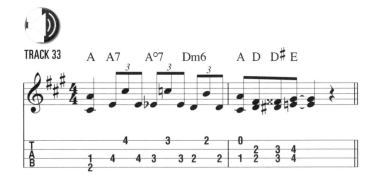

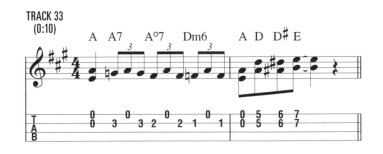

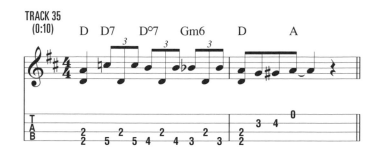

RIFF BLUES

Riffs are often employed in the blues in a fashion in which they're either outright transposed to each chord change or subtly altered to fit each chord. We'll see both kinds of examples in this section.

The following riff is similar to "Rock Me, Baby" (1964) by B.B. King, with sliding 6ths creating a rich blues harmony that lays conveniently in the key of C. Check out how that pesky G string is utilized in measure 9 for the root of the V (G) chord.

TRACK 36

Slow Blues ♩ = 80 (♪♪ = ♪♪)

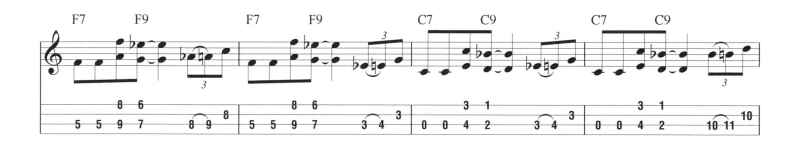

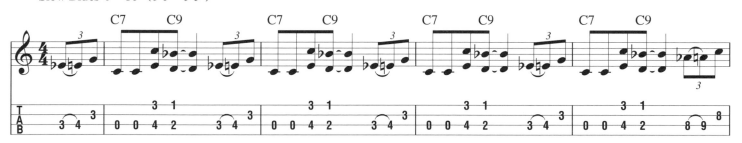

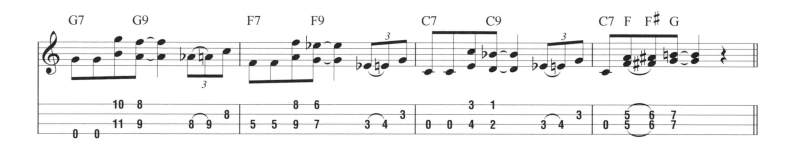

31

Again taking advantage of the uke-friendly key of C, the following classic Chicago blues octave riff creates a powerful effect, even on nylon strings. Notice that the triplet lick on beat 4 of measures 1–10 ends on the ♭7th to emphasize the bluesy, dominant quality of the progression.

Performance Tip: Low to high, use an index-ring-index fret-hand finger combination for the triplet riff on beat 4 of measures 1–10.

TRACK 37

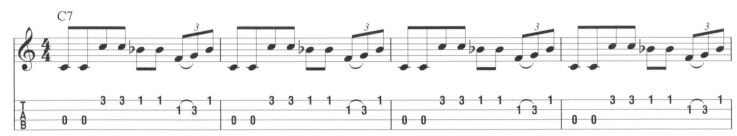

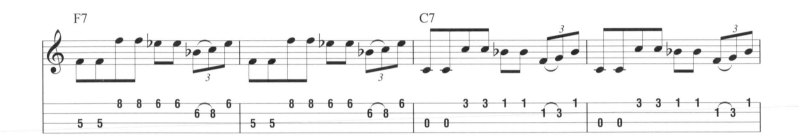

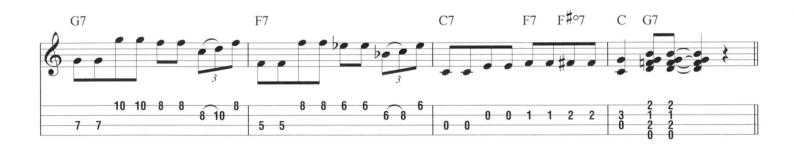

I and IV chords are the heart of the blues and related genres, and riffs involving a quick change between them produce a considerable boost forward. Given the ever-present challenge of the low-volume, light-sustain ukulele, having significant harmony included in a blues riff is always a valued plus. Be aware that various I–IV riffs and rhythms with different voicings have been the foundation of the great Rolling Stones hits composed by ace blues-rocker "Keef" Richards.

Performance Tip: Except for the C7 voicing on beat 1 of measures 2, 4, 8, and 12 employ either a fret-hand index finger or ring finger barre on strings 1–3, adding the higher note on string 3 with the middle finger where appropriate.

TRACK 38

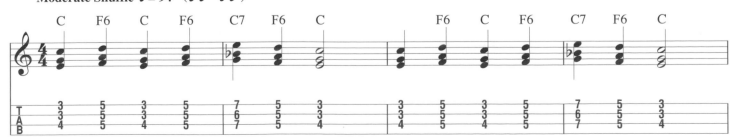

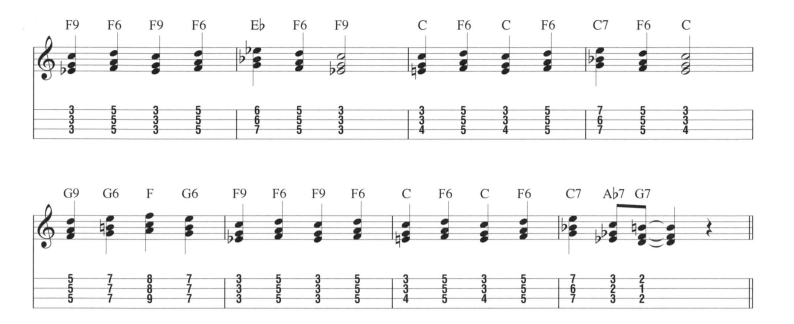

The classic IV–I double-stop lick resolving to the major 3rd, in conjunction with boogie patterns, makes for an exceptionally propulsive blues riff. A characteristic of Texas and Chicago blues, the lick fulfills the combined functions of harmony—a smattering of melody, as well as rhythm—and is so inclusive that it could almost be a solo uke accompaniment.

Performance Tip: For the signature riff on beat 4 of each measure, barre with the fret-hand ring finger, switch to the index, and hammer with the middle finger.

TRACK 39

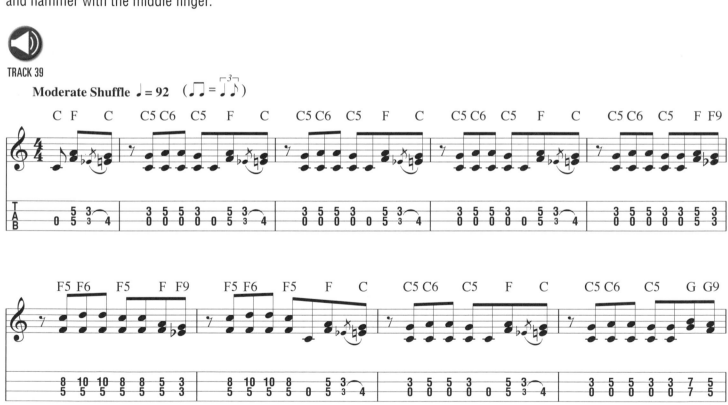

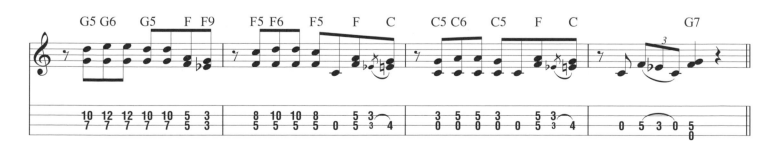

Finding a logical use for string 4 (G), the spirit of Muddy Waters and his two early, immortal classics, "Hoochie Coochie Man" (1954) and "Mannish Boy" (1955), provide the low-down riff on beat 4 of measures 1–4. When the thumping 5ths follow, long roots trail back to the Delta. Observe how a straight, cut-boogie pattern for the IV (C) chord in measures 5–6 encourages the momentum to move forward with a touch more energy for a dynamic boost.

Performance Tip: The signature riff on beat 4 can be easily handled with a ring-finger barre on fret 3 and an index-finger barre on fret 1.

TRACK 40

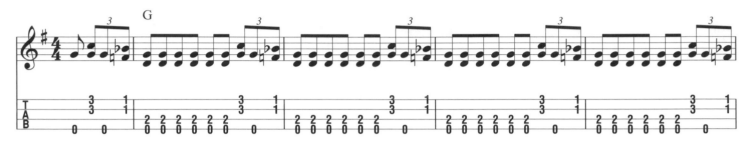

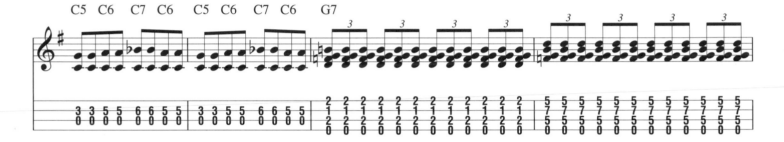

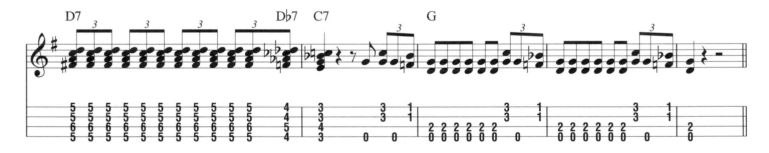

A boogie pattern that is harmonized with chords takes advantage of not only the full, four-string range of the ukulele, but also of its special tuning (i.e., the often problematic string 4 [G]).

Performance Tip: Simply use the fret-hand index, middle, and pinky fingers on string 3 for measures 1–4, 7–8, and 11–12, over the I (A) chord. For the IV (D) and V (E) chords, barre the index finger across all four strings, with the middle finger on string 3, and then place the ring and pinky fingers as required to access the other voicings.

TRACK 41

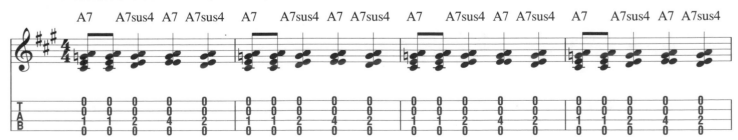

Another variation in the key of E on the protean "Rock Me, Baby" concept incorporates the always welcome and blues-approved sliding 6ths. As opposed to the guitar, playing in E on the ukulele does not produce the same deep country-blues sound. However, the availability of open strings for the I (E) and IV (A) chords, which may be sustained to a degree, is an advantage in this figure.

Performance Tip: As always with 6ths, use the middle and index fingers, low to high, for the dyads in a diagonal pattern.

TRACK 42

With a rhythm similar to Track 32, the following classic Delta blues chordal sequence of the major to the dominant 7th, popularized by Robert Johnson on "32-20 Blues" (1936) and "Steady Rollin' Man" (1937), among others, is a worthy classic to be absorbed. Besides a convenient way to create the standard blues harmony, it also puts the hand in a finger-friendly position for reaching choice scale notes that are located within each relative barre-chord voicing.

Performance Tip: Barre with the fret-hand index finger at frets 2, 7, and 9, respectively, and switch from the pinky to the middle finger on string 1 to move from the major to the dominant 7th chord.

TRACK 43

BLUES SOLOS

In this section, we'll take a look at how the ukulele can be treated as a lead instrument in the blues. The examples are complete with many stylistic techniques, including bends, slides, and vibrato. To achieve the vibrato, you can use one of two methods. One involves moving the string back and forth, perpendicular to the neck. This motion is similar to the way a blues guitarist produces vibrato. It can sound nice on the uke, too, though it produces a bit of noise by virtue of the strings scraping on the frets. The other method involves pushing (toward the soundhole) and pulling (toward the tuners) along the length of the string in a steady, repetitive motion. This approach can produce a nice, clean vibrato, but it will be most pronounced in the middle portion of the neck. On the first few frets, the effect will not be noticeable much at all.

Featuring the C minor pentatonic, major pentatonic, and composite blues scales, with their useful open strings as fodder, the I (C), IV (F), and V (G) changes are "picked over" in the following solo for the root notes and other cool blues scale degrees like the ♭7th (B♭ over C, E♭ over F, and F over G). Check out how the E♭ (♭3rd) on beat 4 of measure 4 (I chord) leads the ear nicely to the IV chord in measure 5.

Performance Tip: In most measures, the fret-hand index finger should be located around fret 3 and the pinky around fret 6 to efficiently access the notes in between.

TRACK 44

37

Besides having the open-string root (G) on the bottom for resolution at the end of descending runs, the key of G for blues is conducive to compact licks for the I and IV (C) chords. In addition, the classic blues "train whistle," which has been a favorite of blues musicians since the era of steam engine locomotives, lays conveniently at fret 5, as seen in measure 4.

Performance Tip: Play the "train whistle" with the fret-hand middle and index fingers, low to high. Execute the harmony bends in measures 9, 10, and 11 over the V, IV (C), and I changes, respectively, with the middle and ring fingers, low to high.

TRACK 45

Slow Blues ♩ = 72

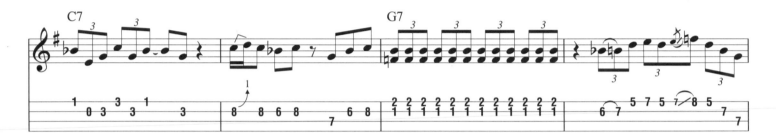

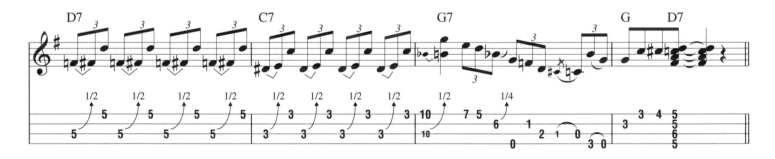

With the open-string root (A) on top, a different technique enters the picture—"pedal point," as seen in measures 7 and 8 over the I (A) chord. Inasmuch as the ukulele is a low-sustain instrument, the ringing string not only helps to fill up the sound, but also contributes a degree of musical tension. In addition, the key of A encourages long, descending (or ascending), easily accessible runs, as in measure 4 over the I chord.

Performance Tip: Play the triplets in measure 1 by anchoring the fret-hand index finger on string 1 and hammering from the middle to the ring finger on string 2.

TRACK 46

Moderate Shuffle ♩ = 110

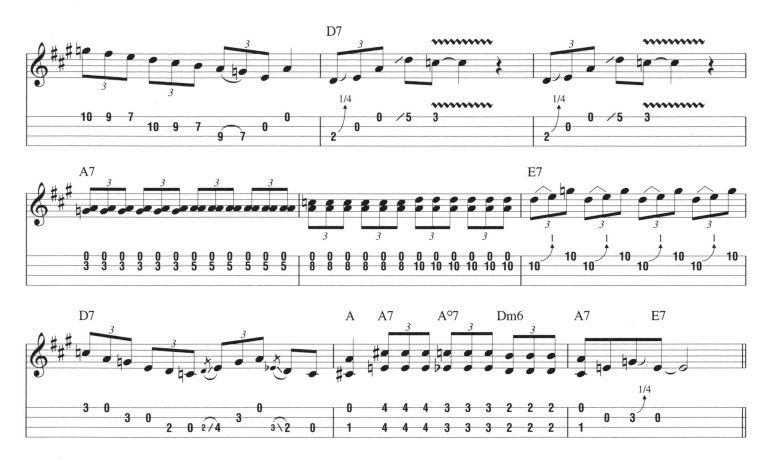

The low-down "country bluesman's key" of E also offers its own unique arrangement of notes for improvisation. Measure 1 over the I (E) chord shows how one position can yield a quick, efficient means by which to run up the scale and extend a musical idea, with a bend as bluesy punctuation. On top of that, dyads lay conveniently on strings 1 and 2 to flesh out the respective harmonies.

Performance Tip: Access the 6th chord voicings in measure 9 (B6 and B♭6) with a fingering of (low to high) middle, ring, and index fingers. For the A6 that follows in measure 10, simply slide down and use the middle and ring fingers on strings 3 and 2, respectively, releasing the index finger.

Slow Blues ♩ = 80

TRACK 47

The following fast shuffle in the key of D clearly displays its desirable characteristics. Essentially a blues "head," it incorporates two classic blues riffs as motifs that harmonize simultaneously with the I (D) and IV (G) chords in measures 1–6 in a tradition that harkens back to the swing era. Notice the ascending composite blues scale runs, derived from the changes in measures 9 and 10 (the V [A] and IV chords, respectively), that help to push the shuffle forward.

Performance Tip: After playing the A and G root notes on beat 4 of measures 8 (V chord) and 9 (IV chord), respectively, utilize the fret-hand index, middle, ring, and pinky fingers for the chromatic runs.

TRACK 48

FINGERSTYLE BLUES

In this section, we'll examine the art of fingerpicking the uke, blues style. Whereas most of the examples thus far could be articulated by strumming with the thumb or fingers, these examples will require the use of several different fingers of the plucking hand. Remember to take any difficult measures slowly until the picking pattern begins to feel comfortable.

In this first example, a brisk, chugging shuffle is created with a riff that implies harmonic movement from C to C7 on the I (C) chord change in measures 1–4 and 7–8, while dominant voicings are plucked for the V (G7) and IV (F7) chords in measures 9 and 10, respectively. The contrasting parts produce dynamic musical contrast while maintaining the required forward motion that continues until the turnaround in measures 11–12.

Performance Tip: Inasmuch as the ukulele is meant to be played fingerstyle, with at least the pick-hand thumb and index finger, it is recommended that the middle finger also be added to the mix for all the fingerstyle blues figures. Whereas classical guitarists tend to follow a rigorously prescribed pick-hand fingering technique, blues and folk guitarists (and uke pluckers) are free to find what works best for them through experimentation.

TRACK 49

Moderate Shuffle ♩ = 100

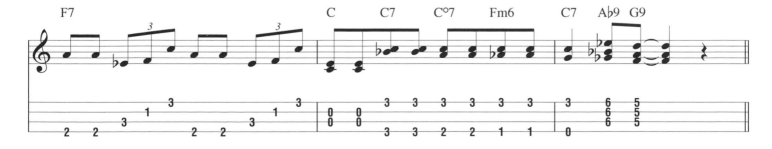

Similar patterns played over all three chord changes are the foundation of classic Delta blues like Robert Johnson's "32-20 Blues" (1936) and "I'm a Steady Rollin' Man" (1937). "Blues Theory 101" dictates that major triads are followed by dominant 7th voicings to ensure forward momentum to, and anticipation of, the next chord change. Check out how the harmonic movement from major to dominant occurs within the V (G) and IV (F) chords in measures 9 and 10 to accelerate the perceived forward thrust to the turnaround in measures 11–12.

Performance Tip: In what is a strongly suggested technique to acquire, utilize the pick-hand thumb on string 4, along with the middle finger on string 1 and the index finger on string 2.

TRACK 50

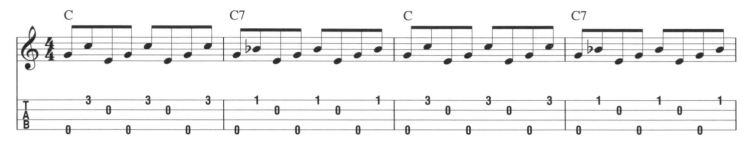

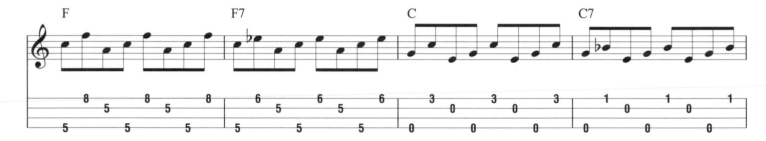

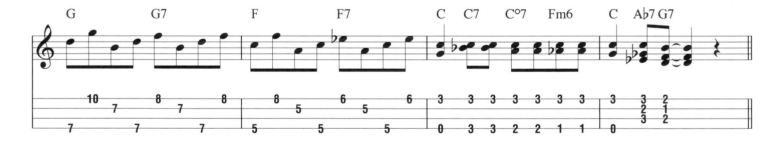

Almost by definition, up-tempo fingerstyle shuffles require steady, driving eighth notes. Carefully placed triplets contribute even more momentum, as seen on beat 4 of measures 1–4 and 7–8 over the I (C) chord, and in measures 9 and 10 over the V (G) and IV (F) changes, respectively.

Performance Tip: Use the fret-hand pinky for the B♭ note (fret 6) over the I chord and pull off from A to G on beat 4 with the ring and index fingers.

TRACK 51

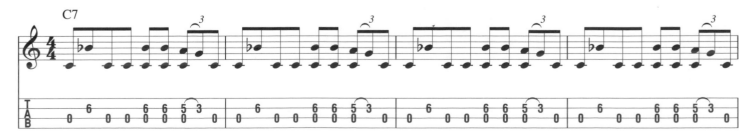

42

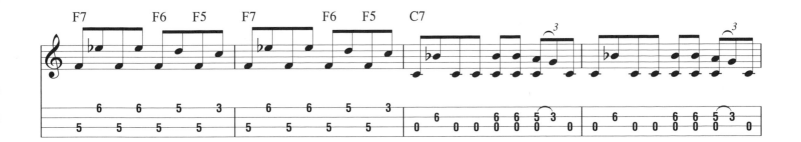

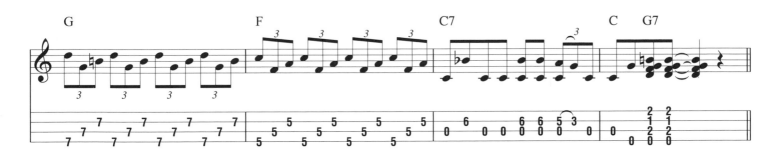

One of the many potent characteristics of country and Delta blues is the implied movement from the major triad to 7th, 6th, or 5th voicings to enrich the harmony. As a prominent characteristic of most prewar and postwar blues, the I (G), IV (C), and V (D) chord changes each contain descending harmony for a dramatic effect. Observe how measure 10 (IV chord) features a different descending harmony than measures 5–6 and how it connects smoothly and logically to the ascending turnaround pattern in measures 11–12.

Performance Tip: Play the triplets in measures 1–4 and 7–8 (I chord) with the pick-hand thumb, index, and middle fingers, low to high. Do the same for the triplets in measures 5–6 over the IV chord.

TRACK 52

The "re-entrant" G string on the bottom presents the opportunity for dynamic shifts in register, along with ringing octaves, in a bouncy, ragtime-type blues. Notice that the figure is notated in straight 4/4 time with a "swung 16ths" feel. Check out the diminished 7th chord on beat 2 over the I chord, which injects a quick hit of musical tension before resolving back to a dominant 7th voicing.

Performance Tip: Allow the common strings and notes to ring whenever possible.

TRACK 53

UKULELE SLIDE BLUES

Though the petite size and nylon strings of the soprano uke tend to run counter to the volume and sustain most often required for playing slide, it is still worthwhile and fun to give it a shot. Be aware that "Walking Blues" and "Little Red Rooster" are the impetus for the creation of the hip Delta "bottleneck" progression below. As in standard tuning on the guitar, chordal harmony that emphasizes the changes is one of the goals, as can be seen in measures 5–6 and 10 over the IV (F) chord, and measure 9 over the V (G) chord.

Performance Tip: A thin glass slide, worn on the pinky, is recommended for uke slide. Though nowhere near as critical as on steel strings, it is still paramount to mute unwanted string vibrations with the left hand by simultaneously lightly dragging the ring, middle, and index fingers on the strings behind the slide, as well as dropping the heel of the pick hand down on the strings near the bridge when needed.

TRACK 54

Moderate Blues ♩ = 132

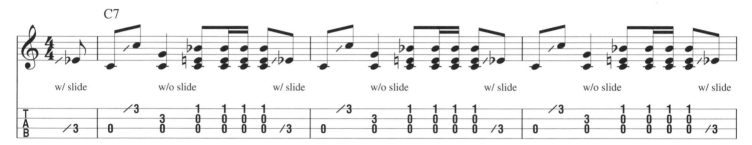

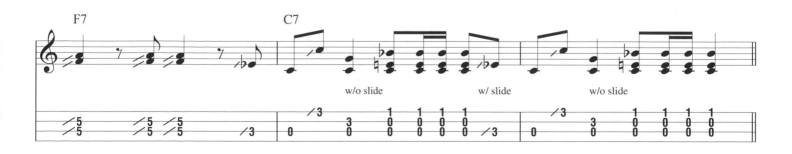

Reminiscent of chord-driven prewar slide classics like "Rollin' and Tumblin'," "Terraplane Blues," and "Crossroads Blues," the following progression brings out the unique ukulele tuning courtesy of the high string on the bottom. As intimated in Track 54, the number one rule for playing slide in standard tuning is to access harmony when desired with the bottom three strings of the ukulele fortuitously providing major triads.

Performance Tip: Pluck the chords with the pick-hand thumb, index, and middle fingers, low to high.

TRACK 55

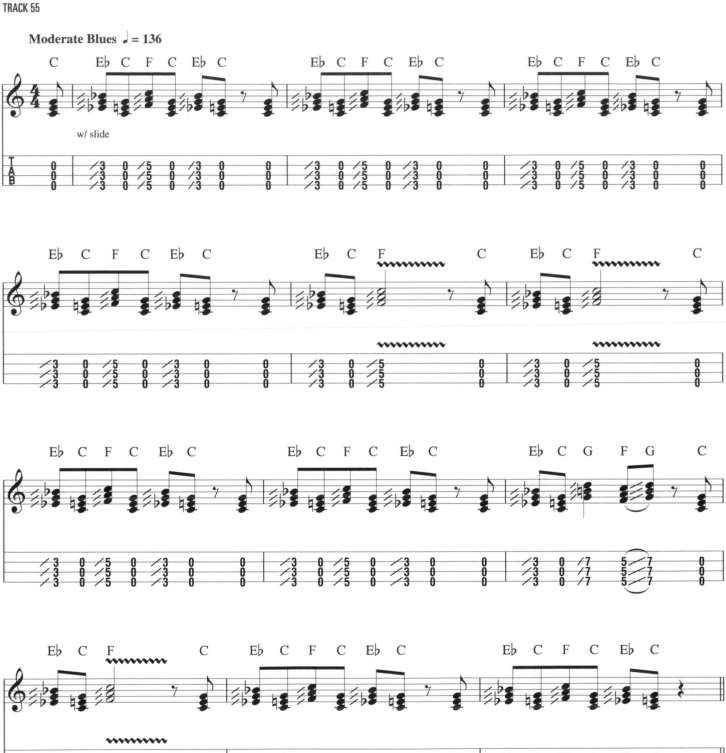

Bo Diddley's modal "I'm a Man" (1955) provides the inspiration for the following 12-bar "call and response" progression that features single-note fills in open G tuning. Know that there are two "soloing strategies" for improvising in open-tuned slide. Both have advantages and disadvantages. One strategy is to derive all the licks from one tonic scale, such as the major pentatonic or composite blues scale. The other is commonly referred to as "playing the changes" and involves changing scales with each chord change. The latter approach is employed here. Be aware that it is not necessary to make one choice over the other within a particular composition—the two may be combined.

Performance Tip: In each measure, be sure to dampen the strings following the last chord before the lick.

TRACK 56

Open G tuning:
(low to high) G–B–D–G

UKULELE NOTATION LEGEND

THE MUSICAL STAFF shows pitches and rhythms and is divided by bar lines into measures. Pitches are named after the first seven letters of the alphabet.

TABLATURE graphically represents the ukulele fingerboard. Each horizontal line represents a a string, and each number represents a fret.

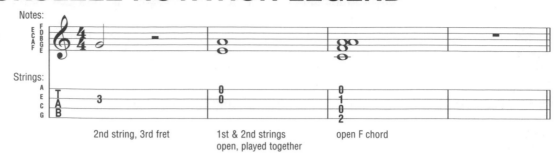

2nd string, 3rd fret   1st & 2nd strings open, played together   open F chord

HALF-STEP BEND: Strike the note and bend up 1/2 step.

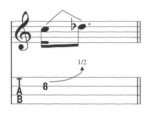

WHOLE-STEP BEND: Strike the note and bend up one step.

GRACE NOTE BEND: Strike the note and immediately bend up as indicated.

SLIGHT (MICROTONE) BEND: Strike the note and bend up 1/4 step.

BEND AND RELEASE: Strike the note and bend up as indicated, then release back to the original note. Only the first note is struck.

PRE-BEND: Bend the note as indicated, then strike it.

VIBRATO: The string is vibrated by rapidly bending and releasing the note with the fretting hand.

HAMMER-ON: Strike the first (lower) note with one finger, then sound the higher note (on the same string) with another finger by fretting it without picking.

PULL-OFF: Place both fingers on the notes to be sounded. Strike the first note and without picking, pull the finger off to sound the second (lower) note.

LEGATO SLIDE: Strike the first note and then slide the same fret-hand finger up or down to the second note. The second note is not struck.

SHIFT SLIDE: Same as legato slide, except the second note is struck.

TRILL: Very rapidly alternate between the notes indicated by continuously hammering on and pulling off.

TREMOLO PICKING: The note is picked as rapidly and continuously as possible.

NOTE: Tablature numbers in parentheses mean:

1. The note is being sustained over a system (note in standard notation is tied), or

2. The note is sustained, but a new articulation (such as a hammer-on, pull-off, slide or vibrato) begins, or

3. The note is a barely audible "ghost" note (note in standard notation is also in parentheses).

Additional Musical Definitions

(accent) • Accentuate note (play it louder)

(staccato) • Play the note short

D.S. al Coda • Go back to the sign (𝄋), then play until the measure marked "***To Coda***," then skip to the section labelled "**Coda**."

D.C. al Fine • Go back to the beginning of the song and play until the measure marked "***Fine***" (end).

N.C. • No chord.

• Repeat measures between signs.

• When a repeated section has different endings, play the first ending only the first time and the second ending only the second time.